Spotlight on
Argentina

Bobbie Kalman

Crabtree Publishing Company

www.crabtreebooks.com

Spotlight On My Country

Created by Bobbie Kalman

For my "sweet" friend Susie Schilling,
pastry chef extraordinaire
Your amazing creations delight all our senses!

Author and Editor-in-Chief
Bobbie Kalman

Editor
Kathy Middleton

Proofreader
Crystal Sikkens

Photo research
Bobbie Kalman

Design
Bobbie Kalman
Katherine Berti
Samantha Crabtree (cover)

Print and production coordinator
Katherine Berti

Photographs
ZUMAPRESS.com/Keystone Press: page 7 (b)
Shutterstock: back cover, pages 1, 4 (t), 5 (l), 6 (r), 7 (tl, tc, m), 8, 9 (b), 10, 11, 12 (b), 13 (t), 14 (b), 15, 16, 17 (b), 18 (t), 19 (b), 20 (b), 21 (br), 22 (t), 25 (tr, b), 29 (ml, br), 30, 31; meunierd: pages 17 (t), 23 (t), 29 (tr);
Kobby Dagan: front cover, pages 21 (tl), 25 (tl), 27 (tr, b);
Eduardo Rivero: pages 26, 27 (tl), 28 (b);
david alayo: page 29 (bl)
Thinkstock: pages 7 (tr), 9 (t), 14 (t), 19 (t), 20 (t), 21 (bl), 24, 28
Wikimedia Commons: Museum of the Argentine Bicentennial: page 3; Djr xi: page 5 (r);
Michaël CATANZARITI: page 12 (t);
Tom L-C: page 13 (b);
Fulviusbsas: page 18 (b); Maxima20: page 21 (tr);
Museo Histórico Nacional: page 22 (b);
Presidencia de la N. Argentina: page 23 (b)

t=top, b=bottom, m=middle, r=right, l=left, tl=top left, tc=top center, tr=top right, bl=bottom left, ml=middle left, br=bottom right

Library and Archives Canada Cataloguing in Publication

Kalman, Bobbie
    Spotlight on Argentina / Bobbie Kalman.

(Spotlight on my country)
Includes index.
Issued also in electronic format.
ISBN 978-0-7787-0863-6 (bound).--ISBN 978-0-7787-0867-4 (pbk.)

    1. Argentina--Juvenile literature. I. Title. II. Series: Spotlight on my country

F2808.2.K35 2013   j982   C2013-900667-2

Library of Congress Cataloging-in-Publication Data

Kalman, Bobbie.
 Spotlight on Argentina / Bobbie Kalman.
     pages cm. -- (Spotlight on my country)
 Includes index.
 ISBN 978-0-7787-0863-6 (reinforced library binding) -- ISBN 978-0-7787-0867-4 (pbk.) -- ISBN 978-1-4271-9294-3 (electronic pdf) -- ISBN 978-1-4271-9218-9 (electronic html)
 1. Argentina--Juvenile literature. I. Title.

 F2808.2.K35 2013
 982--dc23

                                    2013003284

Crabtree Publishing Company

www.crabtreebooks.com   1-800-387-7650

Printed in the U.S.A./042013/SX20130306

Published in Canada
Crabtree Publishing
616 Welland Ave.
St. Catharines, Ontario
L2M 5V6

Published in the United States
Crabtree Publishing
PMB 59051
350 Fifth Avenue, 59th Floor
New York, New York 10118

Published in the United Kingdom
Crabtree Publishing
Maritime House
Basin Road North, Hove
BN41 1WR

Published in Australia
Crabtree Publishing
3 Charles Street
Coburg North
VIC, 3058

Contents

Where is Argentina?

Earth's seven continents from largest to smallest are Asia, Africa, North America, South America, Antarctica, Europe, and Australia/Oceania.

Argentina is a **country** in South America. A country is an area of land with borders. Argentina shares its borders with Chile, Bolivia, Paraguay, Brazil, and Uruguay. It is the second-biggest country in the **continent** of South America. A continent is a huge area of land on Earth.

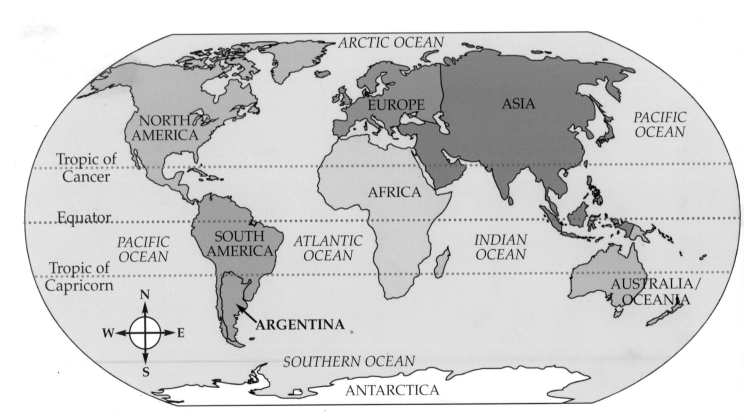

Earth's seven continents are shown on the map above. The Atlantic Ocean touches Argentina. Find the names of Earth's five oceans on the map.

PERU

BOLIVIA

BRAZIL

PARAGUAY

Tropic of
Capricorn

San Salvador
de Jujuy

Salta

*Iguazú
Falls*

Andes Mountains

*Pacific
Ocean*

Cordoba

Mendoza

Rosario

URUGUAY

Pampas

★ **Buenos
Aires**

ARGENTINA

*Atlantic
Ocean*

CHILE

Bariloche

*Valdes
Peninsula*

Andes Mountains

Patagonia

N

W   E

S

*Los Glaciares National Park
(Perito Moreno Glacier)*

Tierra del
Fuego

The Falkland Islands
(Islas Malvinas)

Ushuaia

The map on the left shows Argentina and some of its neighbors. The one on the opposite page shows the **equator**. The equator is an imaginary line around Earth that divides Earth into two parts. The equator is north of Argentina. The weather at the equator is hot all year long.

Another imaginary line around Earth, the Tropic of Capricorn, passes through Jujuy. Here, the sun is directly overhead at noon on December 21, which is the beginning of summer in the Southern Hemisphere.

Did you know?

Argentina is the eighth-largest country in the world and has the fourth-largest number of Spanish-speaking people. Its population is more than 42 million people. Argentina has 23 provinces and one **autonomous**, or independent, city, Buenos Aires. Argentina's name comes from *argentum*, a Latin word that means "silver." Its official name is the **Republic** of Argentina. A republic is a country not ruled by a king or queen. The people elect their leaders. The president is the head of the government of Argentina.

Military leader Manuel Belgrano created the national flag of Argentina.

The flag of Argentina has three wide bands—light blue, white, and light blue. A picture of the sun is in the center of the white band. It is called the Sun of May.

The peso is the **currency**, or money, of Argentina.

La Casa Rosada, or The Pink House, is the office of the President of Argentina. The official name of the palace in Spanish is Casa de Gobierno, which means "Government House."

Most Argentines are Roman Catholic. On March 13, 2013, an Argentine cardinal, Cardinal Jorge Mario Bergoglio, was chosen as the Pope, the head of the Roman Catholic Church. He chose the name Pope Francis I. He is the first Pope from North or South America. The parents of Pope Francis I **emigrated**, or moved, from Italy to live in Argentina, where the Pope was born.

Climate and the land

From north to south, Argentina's climate and land vary greatly. In the north, the weather is **tropical**. Tropical places are hot for most of the year, except high on mountains. In the middle of Argentina, the temperatures are **moderate**. Moderate temperatures are neither too hot nor too cold. The south is the coldest region. Winters can get very cold. On Argentina's high mountains, the temperatures stay cold, even in summer, and there is snow on the **peaks**, or tops.

Iguazú Falls in the north of Argentina is made up of 275 waterfalls. The falls lie along the Iguazú River on the border with Brazil. The horseshoe-shaped falls are more than twice as wide as Niagara Falls! The area around Iguazú Falls is tropical. Forests filled with many kinds of animals surround the falls.

In northwest Argentina, the town of Purmamarca sits below the Hill of Seven Colors. The hill got is name from the colors created by the minerals in the sides of the hills.

The Pampas is a region with huge **plains**, or low areas of grass-covered land. Much of Argentina's food is grown there. The weather in the Pampas is mild for most of the year.

Patagonia is a region that covers the mid-to-southern part of Argentina. It has grassy plains, mountains, **glaciers**, and beaches. Part of Patagonia touches the Atlantic Ocean.

The Andes Mountains

The Andes is the longest mountain range in the world, stretching over 4,400 miles (7,000 km). It is located along the west coast of South America and is part of the countries of Argentina, Bolivia, Chile, Colombia, Ecuador, Peru, and Venezuela. Mount Aconcagua is the highest peak. It is 22,841 feet (6,962 meters) high and is located in the province of Mendoza in Argentina. In the deep valleys of the southern Andes, glaciers have formed over thousands of years. A glacier is a thick, slow-moving river of ice.

The Perito Moreno Glacier is located in Glaciares National Park in the southern Andes. It is one of 47 big glaciers in the park. People from all over the world come to see the Perito Moreno Glacier, which covers part of Lake Argentino. Sometimes pieces break off into the water with a loud cracking sound.

Mount Fitz Roy rises above a plain in the Patagonia region. It is one of the most challenging mountains to climb because of its steep granite sides and harsh weather.

Mount Lanin is one of many volcanoes in the Andes. It lies between Argentina and Chile and has not erupted in 10,000 years.

Mount Lanin

On the Atlantic

The southern right whale spends summer in the Southern Ocean close to Antarctica, where it finds food. In winter, it swims a long way north to breed in the Atlantic Ocean near Argentina.

The eastern border of Argentina is the Atlantic Ocean. Located on its **coast** is the Valdés **Peninsula**. A peninsula is land that is surrounded by water on three sides. The peninsula is a famous nature preserve. Hundreds of **species**, or types, of birds, including Magellanic penguins, flock to the peninsula's southern shores to build nests, lay eggs, and raise their chicks. Valdés is also the breeding ground for sea lions, elephant seals, and southern right whales.

Magellanic penguins like these gather in large nesting colonies on the coasts of Argentina.

Tierra del Fuego

Tierra del Fuego is an **archipelago**, or group of islands, off the tip of South America. The archipelago is made up of the main island, which is divided between Argentina and Chile, and a group of smaller islands. The main island is called Isla Grande de Tierra del Fuego, which means "the big island of the land of fire."

Ushuaia, on the big island of Tierra del Fuego, is farther south than any other city in the world!

The Falkland Islands

For many years, Argentina has argued with England over which country owns the Falkland Islands in the southern Atlantic Ocean. Argentina calls these islands Islas Malvinas and claims that the British navy forced the Argentines off the islands in 1833 and allowed the British to settle there. In 1982, Argentina invaded the islands and tried to take them back, but Britain sent troops and won the short war.

Port Stanley is the capital of the Falkland Islands.

13

Argentina's wildlife

Argentina is a large country with a variety of **habitats**. Habitats are natural areas where animals live. Different species of animals live in different habitats. Argentina's land habitats include forests, mountains, **wetlands**, deserts, and **grasslands**.

(left) The pudu is the smallest deer in the world! Its habitat ranges from rain forests to bamboo forests in southern Chile and Argentina.

Coatis are part of the raccoon family. They can live in a variety of habitats, including hot and dry deserts, rain forests, cold mountain slopes, and grasslands with bushes. Many coatis live in the northern part of Argentina.

Guanacos live mainly on mountain grasslands. They eat grasses and the leaves of bushes. Guanacos are found on high, flat areas in the Andes, as well as on Tierra del Fuego.

The Andean condor lives in the high cliffs of the Andes mountains as far south as Tierra del Fuego. Its habitats are grasslands and alpine **tundras**, which are high, flat areas where trees do not grow.

The hairy armadillo can be found in the grasslands and forests of Argentina. It spends most of its time below ground.

Capybaras are the biggest rodents. They live in wetlands, which are covered with water for all or part of the year.

The Andean fox lives in the southern regions of Patagonia and Tierra del Fuego. Its habitats are mountains, deserts, and forests.

Buenos Aires

Buenos Aires is one of the world's great cities. It is Argentina's capital, as well as its largest city, with a population of about three million in the city and another ten million in the districts around it. Buenos Aires was once small, but as millions of **immigrants** came from Europe to live there, it grew into a huge, wealthy city. An immigrant is a person who moves to a new country to live, leaving behind his or her life in another country. People who live in Buenos Aires are called *porteños*, or "people of the port," because their city is Argentina's major seaport for trade with other countries.

The Puerto Madero Waterfront is a district of Buenos Aires. It occupies a large part of the Río de la Plata riverbank. The newest kinds of buildings in the city of Buenos Aires can be seen there, like these tall office and apartment buildings.

Buenos Aires is often called the Paris of South America because of its European-style buildings, many theaters, and great restaurants. People love to visit this exciting city.

La Boca is a barrio, or neighborhood, in Buenos Aires that is famous for its brightly colored houses. Many of its early settlers were from the city of Genoa in Italy. Tourists love to visit this fun barrio.

Other great cities

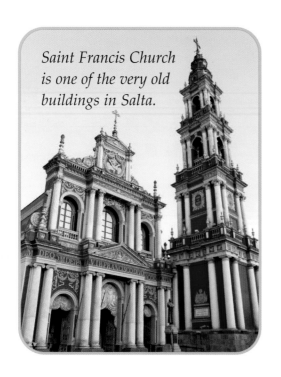

Saint Francis Church is one of the very old buildings in Salta.

Like Buenos Aires, most large cities in Argentina were built in the Spanish style, with a **plaza**, or town square. The plaza is usually surrounded by buildings that include a large church and a town hall. In the center stands a monument to a hero or historic event. City streets extend from the corners of the plaza. Salta, Córdoba, and Rosario are some of Argentina's exciting cities.

Salta was founded in 1582 and has some very old Spanish-style buildings. Its churches, theaters, museums, art exhibits, and many festivals attract visitors from all over the world.

Córdoba is Argentina's second-largest city and is one of the country's oldest Spanish settlements. Córdoba's many old buildings were built when Spain ruled Argentina.

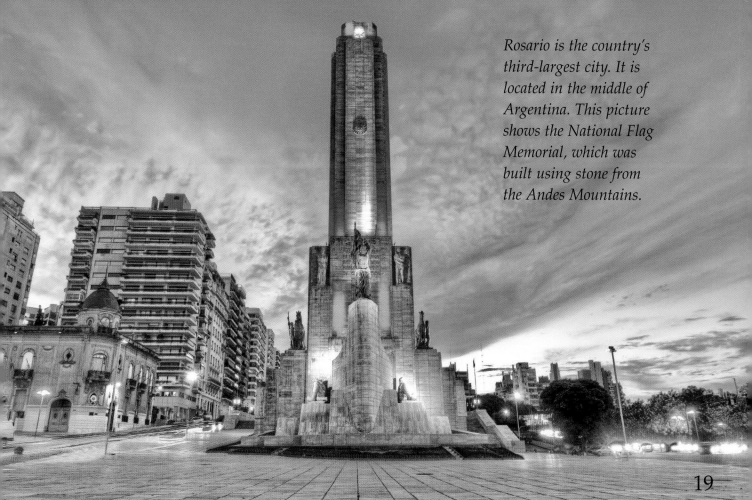

Rosario is the country's third-largest city. It is located in the middle of Argentina. This picture shows the National Flag Memorial, which was built using stone from the Andes Mountains.

The first peoples

Araucano chief

Many thousands of **indigenous**, or Native, peoples once lived in Argentina. Most were killed or driven off their land by European soldiers and settlers. Many Native peoples also died from the diseases that the Europeans brought with them. Although Native peoples who married Europeans have many living descendants today, most of their traditions have changed.

Native people today

The largest group of Native people is the Mapuche, also called Araucano, who live in distant areas of the Andes and Patagonia. Other groups include the Guaraní and Diaguita of the far northwest. Most Native Argentines live in small communities and work as farmers or craftspeople, selling crafts, such as colorful blankets and handmade dolls, to tourists.

This indigenous man is taking part in a gaucho festival (see pages 26–27).

The Cave of the Hands is famous for the handprints painted on its walls about 9,000 to 13,000 years ago! The caves are near the town of Perito Moreno.

The Quilmes people were an indigenous tribe in northwestern Argentina. This picture shows the ruins of a Quilmes town, where about 5,000 people once lived.

Native peoples erected **menhirs**, or tall stones, about 2,000 years ago. Patterns, including human faces, were carved into the menhirs.

From colony to country

San Ignacio Miní was one of many missions founded by Jesuits in South America. Jesuits were Catholic priests who tried to convert Native people to the Christian religion.

José de San Martín was born in Argentina but grew up in Spain. After leaving the Spanish army, he became a leader in South America's struggle for independence from Spain.

In the early 1500s, explorers came from Spain, searching for silver, gold, and other treasures. They did not find any treasures, but they did claim most of South America as a **colony** for Spain. A colony is land that is ruled by a country far away. Thousands of Spanish settlers soon arrived and built homes and large ranches.

Fighting for independence

In 1806 and 1807, England invaded the colony. The British were soon defeated, but by this time, many settlers were also unhappy being ruled by Spain. On May 25, 1810, they rose up against the Spanish rulers and finally became independent from Spain on July 9, 1816. They named their new country the United Provinces of the Río de la Plata.

Searching for peace

Different groups could not agree on how the new country should be run. Civil war split the provinces into the countries of Bolivia, Brazil, Uruguay, and Argentina. In 1854, Justo José de Urguiza became Argentina's first president. Under his rule, Argentina became the richest country in South America through beef farming.

Juan and Eva Peron

In 1946, Juan Perón was elected president. At first, he and his popular wife Eva worked hard to improve people's lives. Later, Peron became a **dictator** and was forced out of office. For most of the next 30 years, Argentina's **military** ruled.

Beyond the "Dirty War"

From 1976 to 1983, up to 40 thousand people were killed by the military in a terrible period called "The Dirty War." The Dirty War ended when a **civilian**, or non-military, government took control of the country. Today, Argentina is a republic in which people elect their own leaders.

Every Thursday since 1977, a group of women in Buenos Aires gather in the Plaza de Mayo holding pictures of their children who disappeared during the Dirty War. They wear white scarves embroidered with their children's names and march to remember them.

Cristina Fernández is the current President of Argentina and the first elected female president.

The people of Argentina

Of the 42 million people who live in Argentina, most are descendants of people from Spain and Italy. Their traditions have had the greatest influence on the **culture**, or way of life, in Argentina. Other European immigrants came from Britain, France, Russia, Germany, Austria, Switzerland, and Poland. Eighty-five percent of Argentines are of European descent. Others are immigrants from other South American countries, the Middle East, and Asia. A very small number of Argentines are indigenous people.

This family, whose ancestors are Italian, is celebrating a grandfather's birthday with a cake and gift.

This young boy has both European and African
ancestors. He loves horses, as most Argentines do.

These young soccer players have
German grandparents, but they and
their parents were born in Argentina.

This family has
both Spanish
and indigenous
ancestors.

Gaucho life

For over 300 years, gauchos have traveled on horseback across Argentina's countryside, herding livestock and doing farm chores on huge ranches called *estancias*. Argentines have an old saying, "a gaucho without his horse is without his legs." Throughout the 1700s and 1800s, gauchos lived and worked on the open plains of Argentina. When millions of new immigrants came to Argentina during the last half of the 1800s, they settled on the open plains where the gauchos lived. Most gauchos were then forced to find new jobs or to move to other parts of the country. Today, there are fewer gauchos, but, as in the past, they still spend most days on horseback.

These young gauchos live in Mendoza Province on the eastern side of the Andes Mountains.

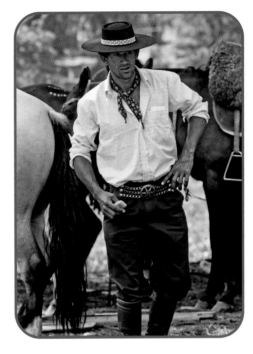

This gaucho is singing traditional songs in the annual Gaucho National Day Festival in Buenos Aires.

This modern gaucho stays in touch with friends on his cell phone.

One of the biggest festivals in South America that celebrates gaucho life takes place in Uruguay, Argentina's neighboring country, during the second week of March. It is called the "Festival of the Gaucho Culture." Gauchos from Argentina and other South American countries travel there with their families to honor the gaucho culture with rodeos, folk music, dance, parades, and lots of food.

Argentina's culture

Culture is the way we live. It is the clothes we wear, the foods we eat, the music we enjoy, the stories we tell, and the ways we celebrate. Argentina's culture is a rich mix of many traditions. The country's arts, festivals, food, language, and clothing reflect the different immigrants who settled in Argentina, mostly from Europe. The cultures of Europe can be seen mainly in the cities. The gaucho culture plays a very important role in the **rural** areas of Argentina.

Pato *is an old and exciting game invented by gauchos. Two teams, each with four horseback riders, compete to dunk a leather ball into a net at either end of the pato field. They try to get the ball away from one another by grabbing a rope handle.*

About 90 percent of Argentines are Roman Catholic. Beautiful churches like this cathedral in La Plata can be seen in every town and city.

Young men in soldier costumes take part in a parade in Buenos Aires to commemorate the arrival of Italian immigrants in Argentina.

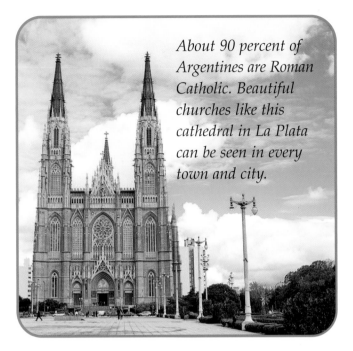

bandoneón

tango

Argentines love music! Their favorite traditional musical instrument is the bandoneón. It is played when people dance the tango, Argentina's famous dance, shown right.

Soccer is the most popular sport in Argentina.

Favorite foods

There are many cattle ranches in the country, so Argentines eat a lot of beef. The gauchos eat nothing but beef for weeks while they tend their herds. A favorite gathering is a barbecue called an *asado*. Families or communities get together at an asado to eat, play games, and dance.

The asado barbecue is much larger than an average one. In an open-air roasting pit using hot coals, huge cuts of beef or lamb are roasted whole on a spit.

30

This gaucho is drinking a strong-tasting drink called **mate** *from a gourd. It is made from the dried leaves of a bush called the yerba mate. She drinks the mate through a metal* **bombilla** *straw, which has a strainer that keeps the leaves in the gourd and out of her mouth. On special occasions, people pass this drink around and share it with their friends. Mate was introduced to the settlers by the Native peoples.*

bombilla straw

gourd

yerba mate leaves

A picada *is an Argentine tradition of serving a tray of finger foods for everyone to share. The foods may include sausages, cheeses, olives, bread, and nuts.*

Empanadas *are pies filled with meat, cheese, vegetables, or fruit.*

A slice of layered vanilla or lemon cake, stuffed with dulce de leche, *or milk jam, is Argentina's traditional dessert. Milk jam is a caramel made from sugar and milk.*

For breakfast, people often have mate and medialunas, *which are like croissants.*

31

Glossary

Note: Some boldfaced words are defined where they appear in the book.

autonomous A country, region, or city that has its own government

civilian A resident of a country who is not part of the military

coast Land that is beside an ocean

colony A country or area that is under the full or partial control of a faraway country

dictator A ruler with absolute power

emigrate To leave one's native country to live permanently in another country

grassland An area that is covered mainly with grasses and shrubs

habitat The natural place where plants or animals live

immigrant A person who moves to another country to start a new life there

indigenous Describing people who are the first to live in an area

military Relating to soldiers or the armed forces as a whole

mission A building where missionaries lived and worked to convert Native peoples to the Roman Catholic religion

plain A flat area of land with few trees

rural Describing areas in the countryside

species A group of closely related living things that can make babies together

tropical Describing areas with hot climates found near the equator

tundra A cold, dry, treeless area that has frozen soil; tundras can be found close to the North Pole and on high mountains

wetland An area of land that is under shallow water for part or all of the year

Index